THIS IS A CARLTON BOOK

Design copyright © 2001 Carlton Books Limited
Text copyright © 2001 Paula Woods
This edition published by Carlton Books Limited 2001
20 Mortimer Street
London W1T 3JW

A CIP catalogue record for this book is available from the British Library

ISBN 1 84222 119 1

Editorial Manager: **Venetia Penfold**

Art Director: **Penny Stock**

Project Editor: **Zia Mattocks**

Senior Art Editor: **Barbara Zuñiga**

Editor: **Sian Parkhouse**

Location Researcher: **Abi Dillon**

Special Photography: **Lizzie Orme**

Stylist: **Lisa Brown**

Production Controller: **Janette Davis**

Printed and bound in Dubai

Neither the author nor the publisher can accept responsibility for any accident, injury or damage that results from using the ideas, information or advice offered in this book.

Candles should be handled with care. Ensure that they are firmly secured in their holders and placed at a safe distance from flammable materials. Extinguish the flame before the candle burns within a centimetre (half-inch) of its holder, and never leave lit candles unattended.

candles

decorating your home
with candles

PAULA WOODS

WITH PROJECTS BY PETRA BOASE

CARLTON
BOOKS

contents

introduction

Candlelight is probably one of the most important decorative devices known to man. However, its creative potential often goes unrecognized. The simple act of burning candles can instantly bring an interior to life – its mesmeric flame produces stunning effects with a wonderful play of light and shadow, and it has unrivalled evocative powers. Even in today's hi-tech world, nothing can rival this living light's ability to produce an atmosphere of relaxation and seduction. There can be no better way to indulge the senses than relaxing in the fragrant haze of a scented candle, and a hot tub surrounded by flickering flames is still the best way to soothe tired limbs after a hard day.

For centuries, candles were the only form of light, their tiny flames symbolizing hope, truth, life, virtue, wisdom and, in religious observance, the love of God. The earliest candles date back to the Roman Empire, when thin rolls of papyrus were dipped in molten wax and bleached in the sun. This method remained unchanged for centuries and is still used today. The wax used, beeswax, was highly prized and reserved for the wealthiest Roman families and their gods, and beeswax candles are still more expensive today than any other candle.

Over the centuries, beeswax candles remained beyond the reach of ordinary citizens, with only the rich and the clergy being able to afford their clear aromatic flame. Until the nineteenth century, everyday candles were made by dipping rushes

or wicks in tallow, an animal fat which produced thick black smoke and an appalling stench. In the fifteenth century a Parisian, Monsieur de Brez, invented the candle mould, but it wasn't until the mid-nineteenth century and the development of stearin that candlemaking changed forever. This discovery, along with the invention of the plaited wick by Monsieur Cambaceres in 1825 and the appearance of paraffin wax in 1850, heralded the end of the reviled tallow candle and the birth of clear-burning, odourless candles that could be afforded by all. The new cleaner, brighter candles were to remain the main source of lighting until the early 1920s, when they were permanently replaced, firstly by the oil lamp and then by electricity.

The term candle comes from the Latin *candere*, which means to be white or to glitter.

Today, candles serve no practical function, but they should still be a part of everyday life. Don't banish them to the realms of the special occasion, instead celebrate their utilitarian beauty on a daily basis. Candles are the ultimate in mood lighting and there is no room that will not benefit from their magical beauty – their gentle glow provides a focal point in even the starkest of rooms, highlighting features and enhancing surroundings. Candles can conjure up different styles and schemes, or infuse a room with fragrance. Their versatility is endless; they can be displayed on the grandest or most modest of scales, but they will always add warmth and colour.

the living room

Candles create instant
atmosphere in any
living space, their
illuminating glow
producing a warming,
welcoming ambience
that enchants the senses.

The living flame

Your home is a very personal place that reflects the innermost you. From the furniture you choose and the food you eat to the accessories that adorn your rooms, everything says something about the person you are and the image you want to create. The living room is where we receive guests, and as such it should be always be perceived as welcoming. The flickering qualities of a flame make it an ideal source of inspiration in any interior, as its fragile light can instantly change a space, bringing warmth and life to a cold room, enhancing rich and cool colours alike, and casting a flattering glow over everything and everyone. On an emotional level, candlelight lifts the spirit and soothes the soul, creating an atmosphere of calm and relaxation that will help to rejuvenate you and your family even after the toughest of days. The most agitated guest will be set at ease and revel in their surroundings, and the simplest of social gatherings will take on a sense of occasion.

Shaping up

Candles can be moulded, dipped or rolled to create a myriad of shapes and sizes, from the smallest tealight to the grandest sculptural cube. Coloured, carved, embellished or just plain simple, the candles you choose will depend on your personal preferences. However, they should be in keeping with their surroundings. Take note of the colours and shapes within a room, and reflect this in your choice of candle. Ornate and intricately coloured or patterned candles may work in more traditional settings, but will look out of place in minimalist, neutral interiors, where the sharp, angular lines of square blocks are ideal, as their simple, uncluttered shape is more restful on the eye. Use long, slender tapers to draw the eye up the wall, or a glass bowl of floating candles to add ambient light to low surfaces. A large moulded candle or a few bold pillars can stand alone, but a small cluster of decorative candles or tealights can be enhanced by using a mirror or reflective surface to double the amount of light thrown out.

The case for the curve

Moulded candles are formed by pouring molten wax into a flexible or rigid mould. Curving, organic, sculptural shapes reflect nature, making us feel instantly at ease. Curves tend to soften a room, so rounded candles are the perfect choice when attempting to make a room more sensual and appealing. They are pleasing to the eye and have a tactile quality that is all their own.

Be creative

Displaying candles around our home is an enjoyable and therapeutic exercise that offers endless creative possibilities. We anticipate the effect they will create and look forward to relaxing in their ambient light. As a rule, a group of candles will always look better than a single, solitary flame, so don't be afraid to indulge your passion. Large candles don't necessarily give off a stronger light, but they can be seen as works of art in their own right, even when unlit. To bring instant life to neutral interiors, set the room ablaze with groups of inexpensive pillars in varying heights. For added interest, trim them with raffia, coloured ribbon or natural foliage tied in place with string. To create an intimate atmosphere, mask flames behind opaque glass. Feminine rooms will benefit from the use of slender, delicately tinted candles, which can be arranged in an assortment of glass or china holders, or try placing a number of delicate beaded nightlight holders on a reflective tray.

Mirror mirror

A simple mirror-lined box makes the most of fragile tealights, enhancing both their flames and light output.

1 Using 25 mm (1¼ in) fibreboard, construct a shallow wooden box large enough to hold a row of tealights. This box easily holds five large tealights. Use a handsaw saw to cut two pieces 40 cm (16 in) x 5 cm (2 in) for the long sides, two pieces 15.5 cm (6⅛ in) x 5 cm (2 in) for the short sides, and one 40 cm (16 in) x 10.5 cm (4⅛ in) for the base.

2 Secure the sides to the base using wood glue and panel pins.

3 Have mirror pieces cut to fit all the surfaces of the box, both inside and out, and ask the glazier to grind down any sharp edges.

4 Glue the mirror panels in place using a strong all-purpose glue.

Making scents

Smell is the most powerful of our senses, with the average person distinguishing around 10,000 different odours. Scents can be used to create certain moods and ambience, and some are a powerful aid to relaxation. Adding fragrance to a room immediately renders it more homely and welcoming. The popularity of home fragrances has increased dramatically in recent years and there is now a scent to evoke every conceivable mood and feeling. Burning candles impregnated with scent is one of the most convenient and easy ways of scenting a room, while the flickering flames help to promote a calming atmosphere. You can also introduce fragrances to your home by vaporizing essential oils in special burners.

Scented candles have been around since the early nineteenth century when, in 1893, the British candle company, Price's, is believed to have produced a blueberry-scented candle. However, it was not until recently that the scented candle really came into its own. In today's minimalist interiors, large scented candles are the epitome of stylish living and are key to the idea of making the home a sanctuary. Although there are many types of scented candle on the market, in general you should opt for the more expensive ones, as they contain more and better-quality fragrance and will burn more slowly. The wax should be softer than that of ordinary candles, as it holds more perfume, and is more effective at scenting a room. Soft wax candles also tend to burn uniformly and so retain their shape for longer.

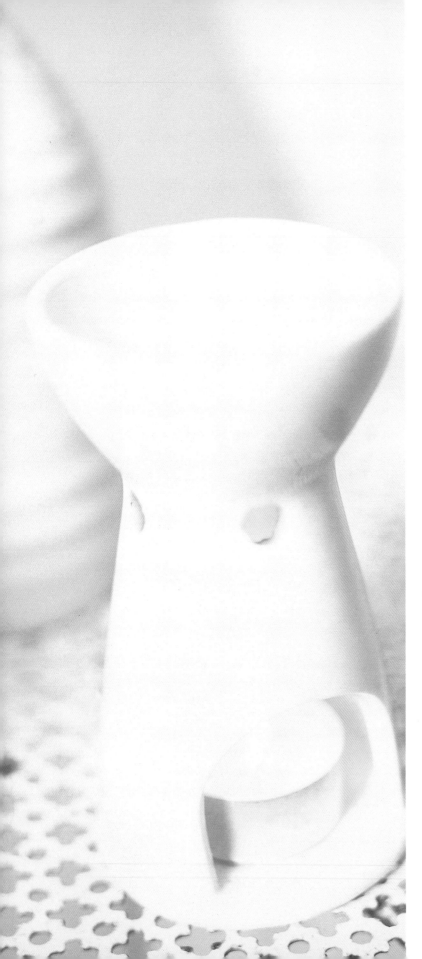

Essential oils can be heated in an oil burner, which comprises a dish of water into which a few drops of oil are sprinkled; the non-electric versions are heated by a tealight placed in a lower compartment. Alternatively, try adding essential oil directly to an unscented pillar candle. Burn the candle long enough to create a pool of liquid wax, then extinguish the flame and add a few drops of essential oil to the molten wax before relighting the candle. The fragrance should permeate the atmosphere for up to two hours.

Essential oil recipes

• For a warming, soothing atmosphere, blend a few drops of frankincense or benzoin with a little rose oil.

• Orange oil is said to banish negativity. For a cheery winter warmer, mix a few drops with a complementary spicy oil, such as clove or cinnamon.

• Encourage lively conversation with a mixture of cinnamon, melissa (also known as lemon balm) and geranium oils.

• To freshen and cleanse a room, try combining juniper with any citrus oil.

• A blend of geranium and lavender oil will help to lift the spirits on a gloomy day.

• Essential oil of pine creates a warm, sensual atmosphere when combined with a spicy oil, such as cinnamon, ginger or clove; and it has the added advantage of banishing unpleasant cigarette odours.

Seasonal scents

As the seasons change, so do our creature comforts. On cold dark nights we wrap up in soft woollen throws. In summer, windows are thrown open to capture every breeze. Candles, too, have a part to play. Light candles impregnated with musk, amber, vanilla and frankincense in winter. During summer, opt for rose, lavender and rosemary to remain cool and relaxed.

Top tips for scented candles

- Room size will affect the concentration of the aroma.

- Don't burn plain candles as they absorb the fragrance of surrounding scented candles.

- Stick to one or two fragrances – our senses are easily muddled by multiple scents.

- Choose candles with a wide surface area, as the larger the pool of wax, the more fragrance will evaporate.

- Keep wicks trimmed: large flames burn scent before it reaches the air.

Colourful outlook

Candle wax is actually colourless, but it can be transformed by the addition of pigment, either directly to the molten wax when the candle is being made, or as a thin top coat applied at later stage. It is now widely acknowledged that colour has a great effect on our moods, and different colours can dramatically change the feel of a room. We are all drawn to warm tones, so opt for reds and oranges to create a cosy atmosphere (although some traditionally cold colours, such as grey and cream, can have warm undertones). All shades of blue, indigo and violet are deemed cool and calming, as they naturally reflect light; these colours may be better suited to more contemporary or feminine rooms. In modern surroundings, use coloured candles as accents that can be changed as often as fashion dictates; in more traditional schemes pick out colours that are already present.

white cleanses
and purifies

orange enhances
creativity, brings
pleasure and
promotes joy

red signifies warmth and passion, keeps us alert and enhances activity

yellow stimulates the intellect

green induces calm, wellbeing and balance

blue calms and relaxes

Sands of time

A large clear glass vase, filled with coloured sand or gravel, makes a stunning container for slender tapers. The addition of a few colourful joss sticks will fill the surrounding air with scent.

1 Fill a glass vase with coloured sand (available from craft shops).

2 Gently push the base of a number of Greek tapers into the sand at random, making sure that they are firmly anchored in place.

3 Wire decorative paper butterflies, flowers or birds around joss sticks and push them into the sand among the tapers. Make sure the decorations are angled away from the flames.

'How far that little candle throws his beams'

William Shakespeare, *The Merchant of Venice*

The chameleons

If it is colour you crave, don't disregard plain candles. White or pale cream candles can take on any colour when they are placed in suitable receptacles. For instance, delicate Moroccan tea glasses, in red, blue or green, will make the flames dance with colour. Paper lanterns and delicate mesh bags will emit a soft glow of colour, while bejewelled votive candle holders sparkle with a dazzling array of hues.

Paper play

You can turn plain glass containers into decorative candle holders by simply wrapping them in paper. Choose a favourite giftwrap or try something more exotic such as oriental labels.

1 Measure the circumference and height of your candle container and cut a piece of giftwrap to size, adding an extra 1 cm (½ in) to the circumference to allow for an overlap.

2 Wrap the paper around the container and glue it in place, turning in the overlapping raw edge for a neat finish.

3 For extra decoration, glue sequins or gemstones onto the paper.

All that glitters

Surrounding a candle's flame with any shiny surface will dramatically increase the light output, both reflecting the flame's glow and making the most of its delicate flickering quality. The simple foil containers of larger tealights can be given a touch of night-time glamour in an instant with a sparkling, colourful coating of glitter. Display them in groups on a reflective metallic tray to further enhance the overall effect. But take care: any glitter that has become stuck to the candle surface may make the wick spit a little, so never leave the display unattended when it is lit.

1 Cover the metal container with a fast-drying all-purpose glue – the quickest and easiest way to do this is to use a glue gun and glue sticks.

2 Sprinkle a thin layer of glitter on a clean sheet of paper and, while the glue is still wet, roll the container in the glitter. Gently shake it to remove any excess glitter and leave it to dry.

3 To create stripes, simply apply a single stripe of glue and roll the container in your chosen glitter. Once it is dry, repeat this process to create more stripes using different coloured glitter.

'Colours seen by candle-light, Will not look the same by day'

Elizabeth Barrett Browning, 'The Lady's Yes'

Remaining neutral

Soothing, peaceful and unassuming, neutral colours such as cream, grey and beige naturally lend themselves to the purity of candlelight. In interior decoration, we all strive to achieve a perfect marriage between form and function, and nowhere is this better demonstrated than in the simplistic, utilitarian beauty of a plain cream candle. For truly understated style, choose all white or cream candles. This crisp, fresh scheme appeals to all and blends perfectly with today's pared-down interiors. Team neutral candles with plain holders made from chunky wood or wrought iron, so as not to detract from the candles' overall simplicity.

For those with a taste for the dramatic, reunite the church candle with its traditional floor-standing candelabra. Made of metal and consisting of a varying number of arms on which the candles are placed, they allow you to display candles en masse. When lit they provide a substantial light source and create a sense of formal grandeur.

Warm welcome

Of our five senses, candles mainly appeal to sight and smell. However, when trying to create a welcoming ambience, do not underestimate the sense of touch. Candles give off a surprising amount of heat, and we are certainly affected by the warmth emanating from these tiny fires. Walking into a warm room is pleasurable; we immediately feel relaxed and uplifted. Although burning candles will obviously not generate enough heat to warm a room, the sight of many flickering flames playing across the surfaces helps to trigger feelings of contentment and wellbeing.

Shining addition

Metal craft foil is the poor man's gold or silver leaf. It can be applied to almost any candle to create a stunning reflective surface that shows a candle's flame to its best advantage.

1 Take a sheet of metal foil and carefully cut it to the required shape.

2 Using a small paint brush, apply gilding size over the area of the candle to be covered with foil. Leave it for a few minutes, until it becomes tacky.

3 Using a soft, dry brush pick up the pieces of foil (a static charge will stick the foil to the brush). Place the metal foil in position and smooth it down with the brush. Do not worry if the metal breaks up slightly at the edges – this will add to the charm of the decoration.

A cut above the rest

Plain pillar candles can be instantly transformed by adorning them with motifs cut out from decorative paper.

1 Using a sharp craft knife and cutting mat, cut out your chosen image from a piece of giftwrap or a magazine.

2 Apply a clear water-based glue, such as polyvinyl acetate (PVA), to the back of the motif and carefully smooth it onto the surface of the candle.

Scents of wellbeing

Along with the flame itself, scent can also
conjure up a warm welcome. Burning creamy
vanilla-scented candles will create an atmosphere
that is both relaxing and sensuous, while church
candles, which contain a very high proportion of
beeswax, will infuse the room with a delectable
smell of honey. Alternatively, candles impregnated
with spicy scents, such as ginger, clove or
cinnamon, will relax guests and stimulate
conversation – as well as helping to promote
feelings of warmth and good cheer, cinnamon
is also said to energize.

Hearth warming

With its ambient heat and light, the glowing embers of a fire make it a natural focal point in any room, raising our spirits and leaving us feeling at one with the world. For those of us lucky enough to have a working fire, the addition of a few well-chosen candles can further accentuate these qualities. In warmer weather, or to simply perk up a false or empty fireplace, fill the hearth with hundreds of tiny flickering flames emanating from inexpensive tealights. Alternatively, opt for one dramatic wax block or a number of strategically placed pillars. The mantelpiece is an obvious and traditional place for displaying candles, but for a novel and more unusual twist, try clipping small candle holders for Christmas trees along its length. Also, consider placing sconces on the wall above. When fashioned from reflective materials, they will not only reflect candlelight but also the flame of the fire itself, creating a warming glow across the entire wall.

Bee natural

Beeswax is a natural product secreted by honey bees for constructing their honeycombs. The use of beeswax in candlemaking can be traced back to ancient Egypt, while there is also evidence that the Romans used slim rolls of papyrus dipped in beeswax to light their banquets and adorn the altars of their gods. The honeycomb wax, once removed from the hive, can either be melted for dipping or cut into thin sheets and rolled up around a wick. In their natural form these wonderful honey-coloured, textured candles work well when they are intermingled with plain cream candles. However, dyed beeswax sheets are also available in a limited number of colours. Although they are more expensive than ordinary candles, beeswax candles burn slowly and with a clear flame, while emitting a delicious honey aroma.

'The normally dreary living room [was] covered with a molten living cake-icing of white fire, all surfaces devoured in flame – a dazzling fleeting empire of ideal light'

Douglas Coupland, *Generation X*

.the
dining
room

The partaking of food
by candlelight is at
once an intimate and
ritualistic pleasure
that feeds the soul
as well as the body.

Food for thought

The sharing of food is a ritual that brings people together in one place to replenish, relax and socialize. Food is a natural comforter, and we immediately feel happier and more at ease with life when faced with our favourite dishes. The acts of cooking and eating engage all of our senses, and these stimulating activities can further be enhanced through the use of candles. There is something about a flickering flame that transforms the humblest of tables into a veritable feast for the eyes. No matter how everyday or mundane the meal, or the crockery or cutlery on the table, the sight of the soft pools of radiant light – like the food – lifts our spirits and helps to soothe away our anxieties. Above all, candlelight instantly creates a calm, relaxing and intimate atmosphere that is conducive to friendly communication and puts people at ease. Whatever the dish, food never tastes better than when it is consumed at a table decorated with glowing candles.

Style council

Candles turn any meal into an occasion and your choice of candle can instantly set the scene. Slender tapers perched on delicate holders and surrounded by crystal-drop collars conjure up glamour and romance; bamboo-trimmed candles teamed with simple bowls and chopsticks evoke the Orient; while pure white pillar candles bring understated style to more modern settings. Metal filigree holders and lanterns bring a taste of the East into your home, and the use of coloured candles will add warmth and ambience to any setting. Even the use of softly flickering hotplates will turn an average takeaway into a feast to be remembered.

Design options

Food is not simply sustenance: the way it is prepared and presented should feed both the body and the mind. When aglow with candles, a table demands attention, inviting those around to partake in its ritualistic pleasure. Central arrangements or rows of candles running down the centre of the table twinkle invitingly and hold the eye. But, be warned, the use of very tall candles may actually hinder eye contact and inhibit conversation. Instead, look for linking tealight holders that snake their way down a table. Alternatively, place a number of chunky pillars in small groups or alternate tealights and food in a row of matching bowls. On smaller tables, where surface space is at a premium, use individual candles to denote place settings; small moulded candles and tealights are an ideal choice. Try placing a tealight in a glass votive holder in the centre of each setting – these can be removed or placed to one side during the meal. Alternatively, carve each guest's name into a candle to create flickering, 'living' placecards.

Edible arrangements

Food is not only for consumption – try blurring the line between eating and presentation by using fruit and vegetables, such as apples and artichokes, to make quirky candle holders. Make sure the fruit or vegetable has a flat base, then simply gouge out a hole to take the candle; place them in individual bowls or group them together on a decorative plate. Alternatively, trim pillars with rows of asparagus spears or French beans held in place with a length of twine, or adorn them with slices of dried orange and lemon.

Floating candles

Water is one of the most romantic ways to display candles. Arouse the senses and whet the appetite, long before the food has arrived, by floating fresh sprigs of aromatic herbs among the candles. Coriander, in particular, is said to stimulate the appetite. If a central display is not feasible, try individual arrangements. A scented candle placed in an ordinary drinking glass will surround the place setting with a warming glow and emit a soft cloud of fragrance. Keep the water level high so the flame burns above the rim of the glass and doesn't crack the sides.

A taste of honey

Hand-rolled beeswax candles, with their delicious honey aroma, are perfect for table decorations. Use natural sheets or choose from a number of colour options.

1 To make the beeswax sheet more malleable and less prone to creasing, warm it gently using a hairdryer.

2 Cut a dipped wick 3 cm (1¼ in) longer than the shortest side of your beeswax sheet. Lay it along this edge and gently press it into the wax. Then roll up the sheet slowly and carefully.

3 Fill a pot with damp florist's foam, then push the beeswax candle into position before surrounding it with single-stemmed flowers.

Floral tribute

A dramatic floral centrepiece or a collection of single blooms brings a freshness and fragrance to the table that is irresistible. When lit, candles not only envelop the display in their warming glow, but also highlight the various colours and textures within it. Candles can either be placed on the table among the flowers or become an intrinsic part of the display. Fill a watertight container, such as a ceramic or glass bowl or shallow dish, with damp florist's foam, then push the candle into position before surrounding it with flowers. For extra security, tape matchsticks or pieces of florist's wire around the base of the candle to anchor it in place. To prolong the life of the flowers, keep the foam damp and regularly spray the blooms with water. Alternatively, simply scatter dramatic flowers, such as anemones, around the base of a single pillar candle.

90% of flavours are actually distinguished by our sense of smell

The perfumed table

A table laden with goodies tempts us with its delicious aromas. Smell plays an important part in the appreciation of food, as it actually allows us to differentiate between various flavours. Without a sense of smell, our capacity to taste would be seriously depleted. Independently, our sense of taste can only identify four flavours: sweet, sour, bitter and salty. To enhance the atmosphere of a dinner party, use candles scented with subtle aromas, such as bergamot, which actually help to stimulate the tastebuds. Beware of heady fragrances, as these may overwhelm the food and suppress the appetite. When entertaining, try burning geranium-scented candles, as the fragrance will encourage lively company, while orange will help to calm and relax. Unscented candles can be trimmed with spicy cinnamon sticks to promote energetic and invigorating company, or add a little cardamom oil to the molten wax to stimulate and uplift the spirits.

Dinner à deux

The sharing and eating of food can be a very
sensual act. Lovers will often feed each other
selected, tasty morsels, and it has long been
held that food is the way to every man's heart.
The romantic glow of candlelight, flickering over
sparkling glassware and fine china, instantly
draws people together into a secluded, intimate
world that is at once soothing and seductive.
Indulge your sense of smell, as well as sight,
by burning candles scented with rose, jasmine
and ylang ylang. These all have aphrodisiac
properties and an intoxicating fragrance that
will help to calm and relax the mind.

Choose candles that will help to set the scene
and create a romantic environment. Opt for
low-level arrangements, as these will allow you
to engage in intimate conversation unhindered.
A simple bowl of floating candles will twinkle
appealingly, emitting a soft, flattering light,
while a host of flickering votive candles will
add a romantic glow over the entire surface.
For those who prefer the elegance of traditional
dinner candles, employ a popular device used by
the Edwardians – candle shades. Usually made
of paper, fabric or beading, these not only
enhance the glow of the candle, but eliminate
any glare from the naked flame, so eye contact
can easily be maintained.

Sequin lights

Small glinting sequin trims turn the ordinary foil casings of nightlights into something a little more special. Group them on a metallic plate or scatter them over a tabletop.

1 Cover the container with a fast-drying all-purpose glue – a glue gun is ideal.

2 Take a length of sequin trim and, starting at the base of the container, wrap the trim tightly around it.

3 Work your way up and around the container until it is completely covered, then leave it to dry.

Kitchen fresheners

In kitchen and dining areas, candles can have a practical as well as an aesthetic purpose. Simply burning unscented candles, and even the act of striking a match, can help to eliminate unpleasant smells. However, the ever-growing market for home deodorizers has seen a vast increase in the popularity of scented candles for this purpose. Candles containing rosemary, juniper or cinnamon will help diffuse food odours, while cleansing citrus scents such as lemon and orange will mask cooking smells – burning a lemon verbena candle is especially effective. Alternatively, use candles that have been specifically designed to absorb cooking, pet and tobacco odours.

An egg-straordinary idea

Delicate, almost translucent eggshells will flicker with soft light when they are made into candle containers. Choose hens' eggs in golden brown or white. Alternatively, try something a little more exotic, such as duck or goose eggs.

1 Carefully crack open an egg and remove the contents. Wash the eggshell in warm, soapy water and place the larger section back in the egg box to dry.

2 Melt a small amount of paraffin wax (see page 137).

3 Place a wick with a metal base in the centre of the eggshell and, holding the wick upright, pour in the molten wax.

4 Gently support the wick on the side of the eggshell, then, as the wax sets, reposition the wick in the centre.

nourish vb. to **provide** with the materials necessary for **life** and **growth**

Celebrations

Throughout history, candles have had an essential role to play in the celebration of special occasions. They herald the coming of a new year; signify everlasting love during the marriage ceremony; indicate the passing of another birth year; and, in ecclesiastical terms, are an intrinsic part of the rituals that rejoice in the love of God. In Mediterranean and South American countries, tapers are held aloft during street processions, and the use of lit cigarette lighters during music concerts (to represent the candle flame) indicates joy and appreciation of a performer. Candlelight can turn even the most humble of gatherings into a magical event. Thick pillar candles will burn for hours, so they are an excellent choice for evening celebrations that might last long into the night, while smaller votive candles and tealights are a safer option for table decorations. Non-drip candles should always be used in candelabras or candle holders, while scented candles can be used to enhance the atmosphere.

Removing wax

However careful you are and whatever precautions you take, candle wax always seems to find its way onto table linen. To remove wax from fabrics, first allow it to cool and harden. If possible, leave it in the freezer over-night. Scrape off any larger pieces of hardened wax with a sharp knife; then sandwich the affected area between pieces of clean blotting or brown paper and press with a warm iron. The remaining wax should melt and be absorbed by the paper; then wash the fabric as usual.

Merry Christmas

The festive season is a time when you can truly indulge your passion for candles. Team rich red, green and gold candles with glossy evergreen plants, such as holly and ivy, and evoke the scents of Christmas with candles containing frankincense and myrrh. True traditionalists can resurrect the custom of the advent candle. This is an evergreen ring holding four candles – one is lit on each of the four Sundays leading up to Christmas, to herald the festive season.

Celebrate in style

• Turn a Christmas tree into a mass of living light by attaching candles to its branches. Use specially designed holders that clip securely to each branch and have a small collar to collect molten wax. These should never be left unattended and are not suitable for use with small children or pets.

• Rich glossy red berries sum up the Christmas spirit: team them with aromatic candles scented with complementary fragrances.

• Slender Greek tapers have long been associated with celebrations; for overhead style arrange some in a flamboyant filigree candelabra. To customize an existing candle holder, thread glass beads onto jewellery wire and wind them around the holder.

• For weddings, keep it simple with white or cream, subtly scented candles placed in sparkling glass bowls.

• Candles are synonymous with romance. For a special Valentine meal, choose pink or red candles impregnated with sensuous aromas such as rose or jasmine. Alternatively, float small heart-shaped candles in a bowl of water.

Happy birthday

A birthday cake, aglow with candles, is often a
child's first experience of the pleasure and ritual
of candles – the blowing out of the candles
signifying another milestone in life. Novelty
candles personalize a party, while non-drip
tapers can be used to adorn the table. Place
them in glass beakers and surround them with
sweets, or arrange them in pairs in narrow-
necked bottles full of coloured sand or water.

Glitz and glamour

There is no need to buy expensive ornate glass candle holders. Ordinary glass tumblers or drinking glasses can easily be customized using nothing more than a length of sheer fabric and a few well-chosen trims. Simply pop in a tealight for a dazzling display aglow with colour. Cover a number of glasses of varying heights and arrange them in the centre of a table for a look that has more than a hint of Eastern promise.

1 Measure the circumference and height of the tumbler and cut a piece of sheer fabric, such as organza, to this size, adding on an extra 1 cm (½ in) to the circumference.

2 Wrap the fabric around the tumbler and turn in the raw edges before gluing it firmly to the glass using a strong all-purpose adhesive.

3 Cover the top raw edge of the fabric with a glittery trim. Cut the trim a little longer than required, turn in the raw edges and glue it in place.

4 For extra sparkle, decorate the fabric with a few large embroidered mirror sequins, gluing them randomly over the surface of the glass.

the bathroom

Candles are a sensual
luxury that will turn
the act of bathing
into a time of pure,
unadulterated indulgence.

The joy of bathing

There is nothing more relaxing in life than soaking in a hot tub. Once simply a functional room and a place for personal hygiene, the bathroom has taken on a new importance in the home. The ultimate sanctuary, it is a private place to which we can retreat to relax aching limbs and revitalize tired minds after a hard day. Bathing is one of life's luxuries; it is an experience that should be enjoyed and savoured, not rushed. To this end, the bathroom should be a place where you want to spend more time. Candles and scent are important ingredients for creating the right atmosphere. The warming glow of the flames help to impart a sensuous, relaxing environment that diffuses the stresses and strains of everyday living. The addition of certain fragrances, in the form of scented candles or essential oils, will determine whether you emerge relaxed, invigorated or ready for bed. Whatever your requirement – whether it's languishing in a hot tub or taking a refreshing dip – enjoy.

A chip off the old block

Sometimes the simplest ideas are the best. A plain block of wood can be used to make a stylish candle holder that is at home in a variety of settings.

1 Using a pencil, mark the position of each candle on the top of your wooden block.

2 Measure the base of a candle and, using a drill bit of the same size, drill holes 3 cm (1¼ in) deep at each of the marked points.

3 If the candles are a little tight for the holes, use a sharp knife to shave a little wax off the circumference of the base of each candle.

Space savers

One of the most restful pleasures in life is to bathe by candlelight, but in a room where space is frequently at a premium, the question is often not which candles to use, but where to display them. Wall sconces can hold one or more candles and come in all shapes and sizes, to fit even the tiniest of spaces. As they are usually placed above the natural surface line, they also help create tiers of light around the room. For a decadent touch, you could also try hanging glass or metal lanterns and chandeliers, but do make sure you use non-drip candles. If your shelves are bulging with toiletries, then utilize the windowsill by filling it with an array of plain or water-coloured candles; gather a collection of glass votive holders or place larger candles on a long, thin tray. And remember that a row of tealights will fit snugly on the smallest of ledges.

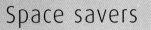

Shore thing

The popularity for decorating the bathroom with colours that reflect the sea or sky, and using materials that echo those of the seashore, make it the ideal place for themed candles. These are candles that are moulded and painted to resemble natural objects, such as stones, shells or even bars of soap. Mix them with the real thing for a truly striking display. These can be so realistic that it may be tempting not to burn them at all. However, they are designed to come to life when lit. The beach also contains a wealth of natural resources when it comes to candle displays. Large flat shells make excellent candle holders, while smaller ones can be used to trim plain pillar candles. Chisel or drill a hole in a piece of driftwood for an unusual candle holder, or simply stand candles in glass containers

Glass on glass

Embellish plain glass candle holders
or glasses with coloured gemstones.

1 Apply a small amount of fast-drying
adhesive to the back of a gemstone.
Press it firmly in place and allow it to dry.

2 Repeat with the remaining
gemstones, either placing them at
random or in a simple geometric design.

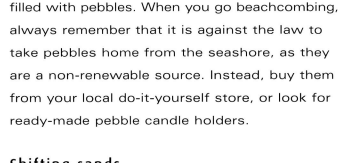

filled with pebbles. When you go beachcombing,
always remember that it is against the law to
take pebbles home from the seashore, as they
are a non-renewable source. Instead, buy them
from your local do-it-yourself store, or look for
ready-made pebble candle holders.

Shifting sands

Experiences are based on memories. To keep
summer holidays alive, fill the bathroom with
tactile moulded candles covered in a rough
coating of sand. The candle is formed by pouring
molten wax into a mould made from wet sand,
which then adheres to the candle as it hardens.
When lit, the delicate flame flickers seductively
through the thin layer of sand. Another idea is to
fill a small galvanized bucket with sand and use
it to hold a group of slender Greek tapers. These
burn fairly rapidly, so keep a good supply handy.

The world is your oyster

Oysters have always been perceived as
a luxury item, and these wax-filled shells
add a decadent touch to bath time.

1 Thoroughly clean the oyster shell
using boiling water and detergent,
then dry it with kitchen towel.

2 Melt a small amount of paraffin wax
(see page 137).

3 Dip the metal end of a wick in the
molten wax and position it on the
inside of the shell at its deepest point.

4 To keep the shell steady, support it in
crunched up silver foil. Then, holding
the wick taut, pour in the molten wax
and leave it to harden.

Aqua aromas

Pioneered by the ancient Egyptians, the fragrant and therapeutic art of aromatherapy is said to balance the body and bring us in touch with our senses. Essential oils are extracted from flowers, plants, spices and herbs, and to date there are over 3,000 different oils available. The most effective way to release the fragrance from the oil is to subject it to a heat source. In the bathroom, the oil can either be vaporized in an oil burner or simply by adding a few drops to hot water. Oil burners are traditionally made from metal, pottery or porcelain. A tealight (or an electric source) heats up a mixture of water and oil, thus vaporizing the highly volatile aromatic essential oil molecules and releasing them into the air. Care should be taken when using burners; metal versions in particular should be handled with caution as they can become very hot.

Perfumes and essential oils can also be added to candles. These not only release fragrance as they burn but cocoon the bathroom in a soft, warming glow. Scented candles are enjoying something of a renaissance, and there are now as many different ones as there are different fragrances. The addition of scent to wax can often result in a softer candle that may have a tendency to drip. To avoid the hazards of molten wax, opt for container candles. These have a special wick that can burn despite being immersed in molten wax. Small moulded candles can be placed in decorative glass containers, such as glass votive candle holders, but sturdy drinking glasses or even recycled jam jars will be just as effective.

The most popular fragrances used in the bathroom are lavender and camomile, which encourage and induce sleep, so are favourite choices for a bedtime bath, and rosemary, which has stimulating properties, making it an ideal accompaniment to a refreshing morning shower. When using fragrances, remember to keep the door closed, so as to capture every therapeutic vapour.

Essential oils **stimulate** the limbic system, which controls our **emotions**, and the hippocampus, the part of the brain that deals with **memory**

Top tips for oil burners

• Less is more: you need only a few drops of oil.

• Always use a plain, unscented tealight and make sure the flame does not touch the container.

• Allow up to 30 minutes for the fragrance to develop.

• Never leave oil burners unattended, and don't let them burn dry.

• Store essential oils in a cool, dark place. Exposure to light and oxygen will cause the oils to deteriorate.

Scents that soothe: lavender, sandalwood, camomile, geranium

Relax

Bathing has been part of ritualistic life for centuries. Both the ancient Japanese and the Romans recognized the benefits of a long, luxurious soak and its ability to rejuvenate and soothe the body. Not for them the quick shower, but huge communal baths, in which citizens would while away the hours. Bathing is not just about hygiene, it should be revered time, when we shed anxieties and relax after the turmoils of the day. When we lie in warm water, the body immediately relaxes and tense muscles loosen – it's the ultimate stress-buster. Burning candles further enhances this process by creating a soothing, comforting light, while scented candles will fill the room with uplifting fragrance. The scents of rose, jasmine and camomile will help to calm the nerves and relax the mind, while geranium will dispel feelings of depression. If you have trouble sleeping, try surrounding yourself with lavender-scented candles or scatter dried lavender around the base of candle holders.

Head for the herbs

When life is a whirl and the brain is on overload, the bathroom is a haven of peace and tranquillity. Herbs have long been recognized for their curative properties. To clear the head, try burning candles impregnated with basil or rosemary while you bathe. Basil is an excellent antidote to mental fatigue, while rosemary will focus the brain, boost confidence and combat lethargy.

The sensual spa

Bathing is a sensuous pleasure and history tells us that it has long been regarded as a forerunner to amorous adventures. Cleopatra always bathed in milk laced with aromatic oils before receiving her famous Roman lovers, while Victorian girls were warned to bathe with their eyes closed for fear of corruption and lascivious thoughts.

For a truly hedonistic experience, immerse yourself in the seductive glow of jasmine- or rose-scented candles. Traditionally associated with romance, their intoxicating aromas calm the nervous system and are also aphrodisiacs. Place lit candles on every available surface – even the floor – scatter a handful of rose petals in the tub, then lie back and soak up the atmosphere.

Float on

The human body is made up of 70 per cent water, so it is hardly surprising that we feel a natural affinity with it. Water is known to soothe the soul, and candles, when combined with water, help create a relaxing mood. Floating candles in water is one of the most romantic and safest ways to display candles. Use glass or shiny metal bowls that will reflect the tiny flickering flames, making them dance across the surface of the water. For added interest, place colourful glass nuggets or a few well-chosen pebbles in the base of the bowl. Where surface space is limited, utilize your bathroom suite. Fill the basin with warm water and float candles in it, then add a few drops of your favourite essential oil or a sprinkling of fresh petals. Alternatively, place tealights on a rack over the bath.

Invigorate

According to the Chinese, running water carries the life force, ch'i, promoting spiritual wellbeing and the rejuvenation of the body. The sound of flowing water lifts the spirits, leaving us feeling happy and refreshed, so no wonder we tend to jump in the shower when we wish to awaken the body and mind. Smells, too, can invigorate, and most shower gels contain fragrances that are renowned for their stimulating properties, such as eucalyptus, lemon and lime. Take a cue from these toiletries and try burning scented candles containing lemon or jasmine to help stimulate the body when bathing. To keep cool and refreshed on hot summer days, vaporize peppermint or eucalyptus oil in a burner or add it to the molten wax of a candle before relighting.

Banish the blues

On chilly winter nights, fill the bathroom with the warming aroma of ginger, which is believed to help prevent chills and be a natural antidote to the common cold. Ginger-scented candles revitalize the body and repel winter blues. On cold mornings, use spicy cinnamon-scented candles.

Quick pick-me-up

Are you bleary eyed and out-of-sorts? Give the body a wake-up call by burning citrus-scented candles, such as lemon verbena or bergamot. The aroma of citrus oils is said to stimulate the circulation and, in turn, increase the flow of oxygen to the brain.

Scents that stimulate: ginger, lemon, jasmine, rosemary

the
bedroom

The bedroom is a
haven of tranquillity,
and when aglow with
candles it becomes
the perfect place for
resting and romancing.

In your dreams

The bedroom is the most private room in the home, a place for rest, relaxation and romance. It is here that we will spend a third of our lives, so it is important that it should be as inviting and tranquil as possible. Candles, with the constantly moving patterns of light they produce, have a soothingly hypnotic quality that encourages rest and rejuvenation. They possess a quality that no form of artificial lighting can match, a mellow softness that is synonymous with sleep and relaxation. If you incorporate groups of sweet-smelling church candles or clusters of twinkling tealights into your bedroom decoration they will, when alight, trigger your senses and present the room – and you – in the most flattering form. No one can deny that candles epitomize romance, and the sensual glow from a few rich, red candles is guaranteed to increase the pulse rate, as does the sight of a loved one.

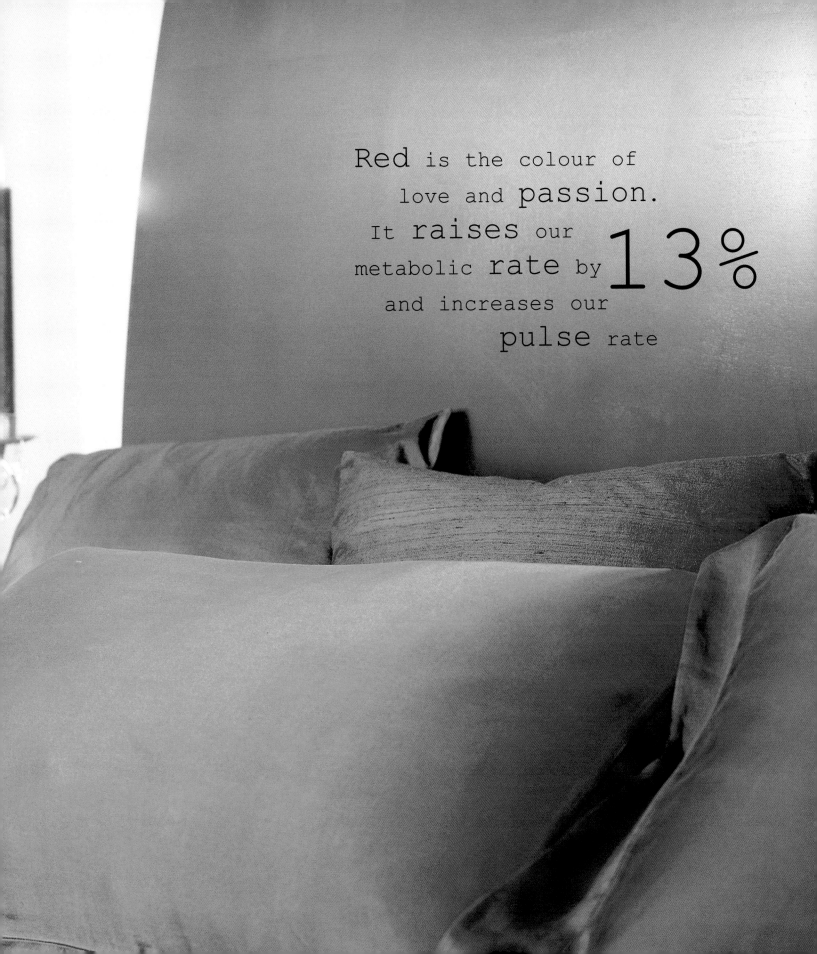

Red is the colour of love and **passion**. It **raises** our metabolic **rate** by 13% and increases our **pulse** rate

Faking filigree

Stencilling can take many forms; here, a piece of old lace has been used to create a delicate latticework design. If you do not have any lace, use a paper doily.

1 Measure the width and diameter of your candle and cut a piece of lace to size. Wrap it tightly around the candle and secure it with sticky tape.

2 Using a water-based spray paint, lightly spray over the entire surface of the wrapped candle.

3 Allow the paint to dry thoroughly before removing the lace. The sprayed design will be fragile, so handle the candle with care.

Would-be lovers (and the art of feng shui)

If you are looking for love, try applying the ancient art of feng shui. Over 5,000 years old, this Chinese art of placement revolves around the four elements, fire, water, air and earth. Fire, which can be introduced in the form of candles, is said to enhance positive energy, while the grouping of objects in pairs – and that includes your candles – will help you find the perfect partner.

Pure romance

The soft light from numerous flickering flames will instantly transform even the most masculine of bedrooms into a romantic haven. The glow from an array of candles is at once sensual and inviting. Arrange them in groups around the bed or place them in front of reflective surfaces to enhance their subtle radiance. Utilize containers from around the home: plain or tinted glassware, coloured bowls, planters, even cake tins and trays can all be converted into a collection of twinkling lights. To add a personal touch, try painting simple heart motifs onto plain candles, or apply a little wax glue to cream candles and roll them in delicate rose petals. Instead of storing candles, put them on display. A bunch of slim candles or tapers tied with ribbon and trimmed with dried rose buds will not only look good but will also radiate a subtle scent.

Glass act

The flickering flame of a candle creates an atmosphere that is both tranquil and intimate. The reflective quality of glass intensifies a candle's romantic glow and also creates delicate dancing prisms of light across its own transparent surface. Look for inexpensive Victorian pressed-glass candlesticks, clear votive holders and delicately etched or frosted containers. Tinted glass will imbue the flame with a mellow hue that instantly adds atmosphere to an environment.

Tealights held in a collection of coloured tumblers in shades of pink or red is the ultimate in romance. Traditional tea glasses with their delicate gold detailing and soft colouring can be bought ready-filled with wax or used as nightlights; they are ideal bedside companions as the flame is safely screened. Alternatively, why not customize your own glassware using glass paints? These are simply brushed on and left to dry. Designs can be drawn onto paper and placed, face outwards, inside the glass and used as a guide when painting the exterior.

Fire and water

With their tiny beams of light glittering on the surface of the water, floating candles have a hypnotic quality that is all their own. Wax naturally floats on water, and these small, simply shaped candles will burn for a surprisingly long time. For a romantic rendezvous, try using a clear glass bowl and delicately tint the water with food colouring, or scatter the surface of the water with fresh petals. Alternatively, place a number of fresh flower heads among plain floating candles. Opt for larger flower heads that will make an instant impact. Gerberas and anemones are a very good choice as they are a striking shape and are available in a range of bright, bold colours.

Top tips for floating candles

• The use of cold water will prevent molten wax from spreading across the surface.

• Using distilled water avoids the unsightly build-up of mineral deposits on the sides of the container.

• The heat from a candle can dull its finish. To regain colour and lustre on smooth candles, buff them with a soft, dry cotton cloth.

• For safety, use a broad-based bowl with a deep or curved lip.

• Trim wicks to around 6 mm (⅛ in) before burning. This will prevent smoking and result in a brighter flame.

• Use glass or reflective containers to intensify the light of the flames.

• Eliminate smoking when extinguishing a candle by gently dipping the wick into the liquid wax.

The power of flowers

Nothing beats the natural fragrance of fresh flowers and they are now commonplace in our homes. The combination of flowers and candles is a classic one, and strongly scented flowers, such as lilacs, gardenias, tuberoses and lilies, will quickly infuse a room with scent. Flowers are also a popular decorative motif in the bedroom. The collections of designers such as Cath Kidson and Laura Ashley are dominated by floral sprigs and big bold blooms. Plain candles can be decorated with simple floral designs painted or stencilled onto the surface. For a special occasion, try placing small arrangements of fresh flowers and matching candles around the room, or decorate the base of candles with a few flower heads. The key to success is to use only one type of flower, so as not to confuse the scents. You should also avoid using scented candles at the same time, as these can easily overpower the delicate aroma of freshly cut flowers.

Budding flames

Enhance a country scheme by trimming the casing of tealights with floral ribbon.

1 Measure the circumference of the tealight. Add 12 mm (½ in) to this and cut a piece of ribbon to this length.

2 Using an all-purpose glue or a glue gun, apply a thin layer of adhesive to the outside of the tealight.

3 Wrap the ribbon tightly around the tealight, turning in the overlapping raw edges and gluing them in place for a neat finish.

Dramatic overtures

For those who prefer the romance of yesteryear, conjure up a boudoir of medieval splendour with gothic-style metal chandeliers, dramatic floor-standing candle holders, wall sconces and richly coloured lengths of tactile velvet and silk. Look for heavy wooden carved holders or metal sconces that feature motifs such as fleurs-de-lys and crowns. Sconces are an ideal choice, as not only do they bring an intimate glow to walls, but they keep the flames well clear of all the flammable materials that are found in the bedroom. This is romance on a grand scale, so be bold. Opt for chunky candles in rich, deep tones, dramatically carved pillars or aromatic church and beeswax candles that fill the room with warming scent.

Floral tribute

For a truly feminine touch, personalize plain pillar candles with small decorative non-flammable fabric flowers pinned at random over the surface (never be tempted to use plastic flowers). Alternatively, for a special occasion you could use real flowers, such as marguerite daisies or violets.

1 Remove the fabric flowers and any leaves from the plastic stalk – these are usually simply threaded onto the stalk and can be quickly and easily removed. Allow for approximately eight to ten floral shapes per candle.

2 Having decided on the position of your flowers, place them on the candle and secure them by pushing a pearl-headed pin through the centre of each flower into the candle wax.

The scented bedroom

Believed to be the sweat of the gods, perfume excites and purifies the senses, so it is a must in every bedroom. It also helps evoke a feeling of luxury. Scents can be used to relax or seduce the mind, and they have long been associated with the boudoir. Using scented candles is a convenient way to marry both fragrance and mood lighting. Many scents associated with the bedroom have therapeutic properties. However, if you are using aromatherapy candles regularly (to help induce sleep, for example), remember that over time we can become desensitized to a particular odour. To ensure that you get the most from your scent and to maximize its curative properties, it is a good idea to change the type of candle you use every now and again. You should also remember that scented candles need to be allowed to burn for a while before their full effects can be appreciated, as no fragrance will be released until a pool of liquid wax has formed around the wick.

Instant scents

If you cannot find the scented candle of your choice, try the following quick trick to fragrance unscented moulded or pillar candles. Using a hot bradawl or wicking needle, pierce a hole, as deep as you can, vertically through the candle on each side of the wick, then carefully add a few drops of your chosen essential oil – either a single oil or a blend – to each of the holes. Once lit, the candle will fill the room with uplifting fragrance, just as effectively as its more expensive counterparts.

Scents of
seduction:
ylang ylang,
patchouli,
jasmine

The art of seduction

For many centuries, the human race has used perfume in an attempt to attract the opposite sex. It is said that in order to win the heart of Anthony, Cleopatra, the Egyptian queen of seduction, received him on a ship made from aromatic cedarwood and ordered her bedroom walls to be covered with roses; she also anointed her body with fragrant essential oils. Today, scented candles, widely available in the form of moulded or container candles, are a much more cost-effective way of infusing the bedroom with what can be very expensive fragrances. Seductive scents include the heady floral scent of rose (an enduring symbol of love and romance), earthy sandalwood and pungent patchouli, which are said to trigger the erotogenic senses. If these fragrances are a little too strong for your taste, try softer vanilla-scented candles, as recent studies have shown that these may have an aphrodisiac effect on men.

Aphrodisiacs

Rose The most expensive and prized oil of all, rose is an anti-depressant and a friend to lovers everywhere. It is said to boost sexual confidence and calm the nervous system.

Ylang Ylang With its sweet heady smell, ylang ylang has a calming effect on the body and mind, dispersing the feelings of anxiety and stress that kill sexual desire. When burning candles scented with ylang ylang, you can counteract the sweetness by placing a citrus-based potpourri nearby.

Jasmine Jasmine has a sweet, slightly narcotic fragrance that eliminates feelings of anxiety and depression, leaving you calm and relaxed. It also affects you physically by stimulating hormone production. Jasmine is almost as expensive as rose, so opt for scented candles rather than oils.

'Call us what you will,
  we are made such by love;
Call her one,
    me another fly,
      We're tapers too,
and at our own cost die'

John Donne, 'The Canonization'

And so to sleep

A good night's sleep leaves us relaxed, rejuvenated and ready to face the world again the following day. Along with crisp clean sheets, plump pillows and soft music, candlelight can be used to create an almost soporific ambience that helps relax the mind and lulls us gently to sleep. Its soft, subtle glow is always kinder on the eye than even the dimmest light bulb and, when teamed with certain scents, it can play a major part in persuading our bodies to unwind even after the hardest of days. Lavender is a well-known sleep inducer. Traditional lavender pillows and essential oil have long been used by insomniacs as an aid to restful sleep. However, other scents hailed for their soothing qualities include camomile, which is both relaxing and cooling; frankincense, whose heady, musty scent promotes a feeling of warmth and calm; and neroli, a supremely uplifting floral oil that helps to quieten the mind.

Sleep safely

• Container candles and votives are a good option in the bedroom, as the flame is protected and the danger from molten wax minimized.

• Never light misshapen or damaged candles as they will not burn correctly and could become a safety hazard.

• Keep candles away from draughts, other heat sources and flammable fabrics and materials.

• Whenever possible, use non-drip candles in the bedroom.

• Never leave the room or fall asleep while candles are lit – extinguish the flame as soon as you become drowsy.

Lavender

The fragrance from this pretty, aromatic plant, with its purplish-blue blooms, is probably one of the most versatile scents we can use in the bedroom. Not only does its sweet perfume lull us into a gentle sleep, but burning a lavender-scented candle will discourage moths and, on hot summer nights, it also helps repel insects. If you are unable to find lavender-scented candles, try making simple lavender candle collars. These decorative rings can be made using fresh or dried flowers. They are more commonly associated with the festive table, when rose heads, ivy, holly and even small pine cones are intertwined around the base of candles. Lavender can be loosely arranged around a moulded or pillar candle placed on a plate or shallow dish, or fashioned into a ring by threading small bunches onto a length of wire. For safety, always extinguish the candle before it gets within 2 cm (1 in) of the decoration.

107

the
outdoors

Candlelight is a natural
living flame that is
instinctively in harmony
with Mother Nature and
is the most sympathetic
form of lighting
to use in gardens.

Outdoor living

The garden has become an extension of our homes, a living, growing outdoor room in which we can relax and socialize. With our busy lives and hectic work schedules many of us strive to re-establish a connection with a purer, slower pace of life. To be at one with nature, whether in the grandest of gardens or the tiniest of backyards, is rejuvenating; it rekindles the senses and brings the body alive. Cooking, eating, relaxing and entertaining are all more enjoyable experiences when practised in the open air. Candlelight provides both a decorative and practical function in the garden, negating the need for costly electrical work and providing a softer, subtler form of lighting than that of artificial lights. When decorating the garden with candlelight, look further afield than the immediate area you will be using. It is not just the patio or eating area that should benefit from the warming glow of a candle's light – the entire garden should come alive with flickering flames.

Summer time

The summer garden provides endless opportunities for candles. Paper lanterns can be hung from trees, while flowering shrubs can be highlighted with flares and a pond filled with twinkling floating lights. Mix candles with natural counterparts: wax-filled terracotta pots look stunning when placed among potted plants on a patio, while staked candles that have been fashioned into flower heads can be dramatically intermingled with the real thing. Dark walls and fences come to life when aglow with simple sconces or lanterns. The garden is the ideal setting for the quirky or unusual, so look in the potting shed and customize everyday garden paraphernalia. Bags, buckets or watering cans filled with sand will hold tall, elegant tapers; while planters make ideal containers for larger moulded candles. Air bricks can be used to display slender candles, and tealights can be arranged in tiny terracotta pots or seed trays.

Day into night

Even on a hot summer's day, candles have a role to play. Scented candles can be used to decorate a tabletop, with soft floral fragrances creating a cooling, soothing ambience. For those lazy days, employ the properties of jasmine- and rose-scented candles to help you relax, while burning candles containing sharp citrus scents will keep you alert when reading and prevent you from nodding off in the midday sun. The ever-versatile lavender-scented candle will not only pervade the air with its cooling, sensual fragrance, but also repel those daytime bugs.

As the sun sets and dusk approaches, the summer garden takes on a new lease of life when illuminated by candlelight. The tiny kinetic light source dramatically highlights areas of shadow and light within the garden. Clusters of scented candles fill the air with heady fragrance, stimulating the senses and promoting a feeling of wellbeing. Lavender-scented candles give way to insect-repelling citronella, and more dramatic forms of lighting, such as flares and torches, come into their own.

Citronella

This fragrant grass, grown in Asia, has bluish-green lemon-scented leaves and the resulting essential oil, when added to candles, can be used to repel mosquitoes and other small flying insects. With scented candles, the more molten wax there is, the more fragrance will be released into the air and therefore the more effective the candle. For this reason, the wicks of citronella candles (and other scented candles for the garden) tend to be thicker than those of normal candles, as this increases the rate at which the wax melts. Citronella candles should be lit at least one hour before the sun sets, as the fragrance will not be released until a pool of molten wax has formed. For the best results, place a number of candles no more than 2 m (6 ft) apart, and keep them lit as long as there are people to appreciate them.

The wind factor

The greatest enemy of the flame is the weather, and balmy summer breezes may bring welcome relief from the heat, but they are no friend to the candle. Of course, any candle can be used in the garden, but to make sure you are not left in the dark, try to include candles that are specifically designed for the job. Like citronella candles, garden candles have thicker wicks than those of domestic candles. These are less likely to blow out, but do result in a faster burning time.

Well contained

Container candles not only have extra-thick wicks, but also provide physical protection for a candle's delicate flame. Made from ordinary paraffin wax, which can be unscented or impregnated with an infinite variety of fragrances, container candles emit a soft halo of light that is ideal for illuminating tables, low walls, windowsills and even shadowy steps. Although there are a huge variety of container candles on the

market, usually fashioned from pottery or glass, you can easily make your own using terracotta plant pots – the older and more weathered they are the better. You can add a wick and molten wax to the pot (see page 137), or drop in a moulded candle. To emphasize the reflective qualities of the flame, try painting the inside of the pot with a shiny metallic paint.

By the light of the lamp

Legend has it that it was Alfred the Great who devised the earliest form of lantern in the ninth century. In an attempt to shield the flame from draughts, he placed a thin piece of horn around a candle. In today's modern homes, draughts have been virtually eliminated, however it is in the great outdoors that lanterns really come into their own. In the Orient, delicately painted paper lanterns have been used for centuries to protect the fragile flame from the elements, while during Mexican fiestas participants carry lit candles encased in long-stemmed goblets. Traditionally, lanterns take the form of a metal frame into which glass panels are fitted. Today, glass hurricane lamps, metal filigree lanterns, paper lanterns, even mesh bags can all be used to protect a candle's flame, each receptacle creating its own unique patterns of light. Alternatively, create your own lanterns using tealights placed in glass jars – these can be simply set on a surface or wired to hang in shrubs or trees. Leave them plain or adorn them with glass beads or sequins that will transform the flame into rays of flickering coloured light.

Beaded lanterns

Recycle those empty jars and turn them into a delicate string of patio lights – ideal for a summer party.

1 Measure the circumference of the rim of the jar, add the length of the required handle, plus an additional 5 cm (2 in), then cut a piece of jewellery wire to this length.

2 Tie a loose knot at one end of the wire and thread on assorted beads. Leave a little bare wire at the other end and tie it in a loose knot.

3 Wrap one end of the beaded wire around the rim of the jar and secure it by twisting the end tightly around the loose length of wire, where it meets.

4 Bend the remaining wire to form a handle, and secure the end by twisting it tightly around the beaded wire wrapped around the top of the jar.

Edible lanterns

Pumpkin and squash lanterns are traditionally the domain of the Halloween celebration. However, when carved into delicate perforated designs, they can also be used to create stunning seasonal displays. Group smaller squashes together to make a living centrepiece, and use larger pumpkins at eye level on a wall or windowsill. These natural lanterns work on the principle that a candle requires oxygen to breathe. By carving open designs on the outer casing, the air can flow around the candle, while the light shines out, casting a soft, warming glow into the night.

alfresco: derived

from the Italian

for 'in the cool'

Nuts about candles

With a little imagination almost anything can be used to hold a candle.

1 Using a hacksaw, carefully saw off the top of a coconut and use a sharp knife to hollow out the contents.

2 Wash the inside of the coconut shell thoroughly before placing a small candle inside. If the coconut is wobbly, saw a small amount off its base.

Top tips for container candles

• The sides and base of the container may become hot, so always place on a heat-resistant surface.

• Store in a cool, dry place – exposure to moisture hinders relighting.

• Do not allow wick trimmings, matches or carbon deposits to gather in the wax pool, as they not only affect the performance of the candle, but are also a fire hazard.

• To maintain an even burn, centre fallen wicks using a pencil. This will also prevent the flame touching the sides of the container.

Wax lanterns

Hollow candles are an ideal
choice for the garden as they
are, in essence, natural lanterns.
Usually round or square, they
are available in a wide range
of colours, and are often
delicately scented. As the
candle burns, the flame drops
below the rim of the candle,
protecting it from any wind.
Although the central wax area
melts, a hard outer casing of
wax remains, so that the flame
glows beguilingly through the
delicate outer shell. Despite
there being little danger of
spillage from the wax pool,
you should always place
hollow candles on a heatproof
surface, as the base may
become very hot and, after
extended use, will eventually
melt. Larger designs can be
used to adorn walls or ledges,
while a number of smaller
candles make an effective table
decoration. Try arranging them
in single file down the length
of your table, or cluster them
together in various heights and
sizes.To extend the life of wax
lanterns, pop a tealight into the
base of the burnt-out candle.

Flames with flare

Garden flares and torches are an ideal way to add height to your lighting scheme; they may also shed a larger light pool than standard candles. Torches, or lawn candles as they are sometimes known, consist of a long or twisted candle moulded around the tip of a stick, which can be pushed into the earth. They will burn for up to three hours, depending on the wind, and are often impregnated with citronella. Flares use paraffin oil to produce their flame and, unlike candles, can be used time and again by simply topping up the container with oil. Flares and torches are especially effective when intermingled with foliage, as they illuminate greenery and create isolated spots of colour.

Come on over

Long, warm summer evenings are all about relaxing with friends and family. Even the most spontaneous of parties can take on a sense of occasion with the addition of a few well-placed candles. Make sure your guests are treated to a light display even as they approach your home. Paths and driveways can be illuminated by an avenue of twinkling lights, reminiscent of a torchlight procession. Use candle flares, or small tealights placed in paper bags weighted with sand, to line dark pathways or guide the way to the party area. Areas within the garden set aside for eating, dancing and relaxing can be denoted using different coloured candles and holders.

Never forget the dangers a darkened garden can bring: use candles creatively to signify problem areas. Large container candles can be used to highlight a steep step, lanterns hung in a tree will illuminate overhanging branches, and flares are ideal for marking changes in surfaces.

To get the tastebuds tingling, draw attention to the delights on offer by scattering the table with clusters of small glass votive candle holders or dramatic container candles, which are less likely to be knocked over than candlesticks. Use candles scented with delicate aromas that are in harmony with nature, such as floral or herby scents. Warming vanilla-scented candles will make people feel at ease, while citronella candles will help prevent your guests from becoming the meal.

In the can

Use ordinary household tins to make decorative candle holders.

1 Fill a clean can with water and place it in the freezer overnight.

2 Rest the can on a towel so it doesn't slip, and use a bradawl and hammer to punch rows of holes through the tin.

3 When the ice has melted, dry the can and paint it using enamel paint.

Concrete tealights

A host of tealights can be contained within a simple home-made block.

1 To make a mould, cut a base of 25 mm (1¼ in) fibreboard to your chosen size. Cut four batons to surround it, allowing for the thickness of the wood.

2 Screw the batons to the base, butting them together at the corners. Then screw the batons together at each joint.

3 Mix fast-drying cement, following the manufacturer's instructions, and pour it into the mould. When it is semi-firm, press holes into it using a tealight. Leave it to dry before unscrewing the mould.

candlemaking

The chandler's art is unique, and there are few things more satisfying than creating and personalizing your own candles.

The raw materials

Waxes, wicks and colorants all combine to create the purest of light sources. The materials of the chandler may have been refined over the years, but the fundamental requirements remain the same – wax to which fragrance and colour can be added, and a wick to allow the candle to burn. The increasing popularity of candlemaking as a craft activity means that all the materials needed are now readily available to buy from either specialist shops or by mail order.

Paraffin wax

Colourless and odourless, paraffin wax is the staple material of candlemaking. A by-product of the oil-refining industry, it is available in pellet or bead form, and melts at a temperature of between 40 and 70°C.

Beeswax

A totally natural product, sweet-smelling beeswax is available in pellets in shades of honey-yellow or bleached white. As it is rather expensive, beeswax is usually mixed with paraffin wax to produce candles of improved quality and with a longer burning time. Beeswax does tend to be rather sticky, so if you use more than 10 per cent when making moulded candles, you must add a releasing agent to prevent the candles from sticking to the mould.

Beeswax sheets

Beeswax honeycomb sheets are available in a limited number of colours, as well as natural honey-yellow. Like the pellets, they too have a warm honey aroma. The flat sheets are ideal for making rolled candles, as they require no heat source to melt them, although it is a good idea to soften them with a hairdryer (see page 39).

Stearin

This acts a shrinking agent when added to paraffin wax and enables the set candle to be easily released from a mould. It also prevents candles from dripping. The stearin should be added to the wax in liquid form. If you are making coloured candles, always add the dye to the melted stearin before introducing the wax. As a general rule, you will need to use one part of stearin to every ten parts of wax.

Wicks

Made from braided cotton, wicks come in range of thicknesses and are sized according to the diameter of the candle – for example, when making a candle 3 cm (1 in) in diameter, you will need to use a 3 cm (1 in) wick. When making floating or container candles, always use a wick specifically designed for that

Wax glue

This soft, sticky wax is used to glue pieces of wax together, or to add wax and other decorations to the surface of candles. The glue comes in block form and only a small amount is required. Simply melt it and apply it to the candle using a paint brush (see page 99).

The equipment

All candlemaking, with the exception of rolling sheets of beeswax, requires a heat source. The wax is melted to high temperatures before being dipped or moulded into the kinetic light sources we so prize. Although there is a wide range of professional equipment available from specialized suppliers, many of the items required can be improvised using everyday household objects.

Double boiler (baine-marie)

This is an essential tool in candlemaking. Ideally made from stainless steel or aluminium, the double boiler (baine-marie) prevents the molten wax from coming into contact with direct heat, and so possibly over-heating and igniting. Water is placed in the bottom pan and the wax is melted in the top pan. Great care should be taken to never allow the bottom pan to boil dry. A home-made alternative would be to use two saucepans placed one inside the other.

Dipping can

This tall cylindrical can holds molten wax and is used for dipping candles. It should be stood in a large pan of simmering water with the water level as high up the sides of the dipping can as possible. The pan of water should never be allowed to boil dry. A home-made alternative is to use a large, tall food can.

purpose. With the exception of those for dipped candles, most wicks must be primed prior to use. This is done by leaving the wick to soak in melted paraffin wax for a few minutes. Once coated, it should be laid out straight on greaseproof paper and left to harden.

Wick sustainers

These small metal discs are used to anchor wicks in place in the centre of container candles. One end of the wick is pushed into the metal disc, which then sits flush on the base of the container.

Wax dye

Available in disc or powder form, dyes are dissolved in stearin before being added to the wax. The more dye that is added to the wax, the deeper the intensity of colour that can be achieved.

Wax thermometer

When making candles, it is important that the molten wax is heated to the correct temperature. The scale of a wax thermometer is 38°C (100°F) to 108°C (226°F).

Wicking needles

Made of steel and varying in size, these are used to insert wicks, and to support wicks in a mould.

Moulds

Moulds are available in an infinite variety of shapes and sizes, and can be made from rubber, plastic, metal or glass. Plastic and rubber have a more limited life than glass or metal, but they do tend to be less expensive. Rigid moulds are an excellent choice for beginners, while flexible moulds allow you to create far more intricate designs. Care should be taken when washing and drying moulds after use.

Mould seal

Mould seal is a reusable putty-like compound that seals the wick in the mould and prevents the molten wax from escaping.

Measuring jug

When moulding candles it is essential to know how much wax you need to melt in order to completely fill the mould. To calculate this, fill the mould with water and pour it into a measuring jug – for every 10 cc of water you will need 9 g (½ oz) of cold wax.

Knife

A good sharp craft knife can be used to cut wicks and trim beeswax sheets to size. A knife will also give you a cleaner line than scissors when cutting stencils and templates for candles.

Wooden spoon

Although wax does not require stirring when it is melting, you will need a spoon to stir in any dye, or when mixing dye and stearin.

The art of candlemaking

Part of the allure of candles is the simplicity and beauty of their form. The practice of dipping candles has remained virtually unchanged for centuries and the resulting elegant, slender tapers add a nostalgic and stylish touch to interiors. The advent of the mould and the discovery of stearin heralded the birth of the shaped candle, which can be any size or form. These are created using a rigid or flexible mould made from a variety of materials. However, the amateur chandler may find rigid moulds an easier starting point than their more complex, flexible counterparts.

Dipping candles

paraffin wax • wicks • dipping can • saucepan • spoon • wax thermometer • wax dye (optional) • craft knife

1 Pour the wax into a dipping can and place it in a pan of simmering water. Heat the wax until it has melted and reached a temperature of 70°C (158°F). At this point, reduce the heat so that the wax remains constant at this temperature.

2 If adding dye, crush it into a powder and add it to the molten wax. Stir thoroughly until it has melted.

3 Take a length of wick and fold it in half. Holding the centre point, dip the two ends into the molten wax, so that their entire lengths are submerged (for safety, make sure that at least 5 cm (2 in) on either side of your fingers remain uncovered). Dip for a few seconds before removing it and hanging it up to dry for a few minutes.

4 Once it is dry, repeat the dipping and setting process to build up the candles to the required diameter – this can take between 15 and 30 dips. If surface wrinkles appear during the dipping, you are not allowing the candles enough time to dry between dips.

Twisting candles

dipped candle • rolling pin

1 Place a newly dipped candle – one that is still warm and malleable – on a clean, flat surface and, using a rolling pin, gently flatten it until it is approximately 6 mm (⅛ in) thick along most of its length. Leave a 1 cm (¼ in) section at the base unflattened, as you will need this to fit it into a candle holder.

2 Holding the candle at both ends, between your thumb and forefingers, keep the base steady with one hand, while gently twisting the candle with the other. Work quickly while the wax is still warm, then hang the twisted candle up to cool.

Moulding candles

rigid mould • primed wick • mould seal • wicking needle • double boiler • measuring jug • scales • paraffin wax • stearin • wax dye (optional) • spoon • wax thermometer • ladle

1 Thread one end of a primed wick through the hole in the base of the empty candle mould. Place a wicking needle horizontally across the top of the mould, making sure it is in the centre, then tie the other end of the wick to the centre of the needle.

2 Pull the wick taut at the base of the mould, and press a large blob of mould seal around the wick and over the hole to secure it.

3 Having calculated the amount of wax required to fill the mould, weigh out the wax and stearin. Fill the double boiler (baine-marie) with water and heat it until it is simmering. Place the stearin in the top part of the boiler and add powdered dye, if required. Stir until the mixture has melted and blended, then add the wax. Heat it until it has melted and reached a temperature of 93°C (199°F).

4 Remove the wax from the heat and, using a ladle, immediately transfer it to the mould. Once full, tap the sides of the mould to release any air bubbles and set it aside until the wax has set. To release the candle from the mould, remove the mould seal and wicking needle, then gentle slide from it the mould.

Adding scents

Scented candles are a luxury we can all afford and, as paraffin wax has hardly any smell of its own, special wax perfumes or essential oils can easily be added during the candlemaking process. You should, however, avoid using oils in plastic moulds as they can cause irreparable damage. Alternatively, the wick can be scented by adding a few drops of fragrance to the wax you are using to prime the wick. Once dry, the wick and unscented wax can be used to make a candle in the usual manner. Only a little perfume wax or a few drops of essential oil are required to scent a candle.

When you are dipping candles, scent should be added to the wax when it reaches 70°C (158°F). Stir thoroughly to disperse the oil or until the wax perfume melts.

When you are moulding candles, the scent should be added prior to the wax, along with the stearin and any wax dye. Stir thoroughly until all the ingredients have melted and blended, then add the wax as usual.

Embellishing candles

Customizing candles is both pleasurable and personal. There is nothing more satisfying than taking a plain object and transforming it into a miniature work of art. There are no hard-and-fast rules: all that is required is a little imagination. Melted dyed wax or water-based paints can be used to hand-paint, stencil or even stamp designs. Beads, sequins, fruit, flowers and wax motifs can all be added using wax glue; and delicately carved designs can be inscribed on candles coated with a contrasting top coat. Newly decorated candles can either be left bare, or protected by dipping or rolling in a thin coat of colourless molten paraffin wax.

Hand-painted candles

plain candle • cloth • water-based paint • fine paint brush • masking tape

1 Prepare the surface by wiping the candle with a damp cloth and leaving it to dry. This will make sure that the paint adheres to the surface.

2 Working your way around the candle and, making sure you do not smudge any areas you have already worked on, carefully paint on your chosen design using a fine paint brush.

3 To make sure you maintain crisp, clean lines when you are working on geometric designs, mask off the areas to be painted using tape.

Stencilled candles

plain candle • water-based paint • stencil • scrap paper • stencil brush • spray adhesive

1 Lightly spray the back of your stencil with adhesive and place it in position on the candle. Press it firmly to make sure all the edges of the stencil are in close contact with the surface of the candle.

2 Dip the brush in a little paint and remove any excess on scrap paper. Apply the paint through the stencil using a gentle stabbing motion rather than brushing the paint. Work from the outside of the stencil in, to prevent any paint seeping under the cut edge and blurring the finished image.

3 Carefully remove the stencil and leave the paint to dry completely before repositioning the stencil and repeating the process.

Stamped candles

plain straight-sided candle • water-based paint • stamp • paint brush • scrap paper

1 If you have not stamped before, it is a good idea to practise on a piece of scrap paper before beginning work on your candle. Brush a thin, even layer of paint all over the surface of the stamp.

2 Press the stamp firmly onto the candle, using a slight rocking motion to make sure all areas of the stamp come into contact with the candle's surface. Remove the stamp cleanly and allow the paint to dry.

3 Reapply another coat of paint to the stamp and repeat the process. Continue stamping until your chosen design is complete, applying another coat of paint to the stamp each time to make sure each motif has the same colour density.

Carved candles

colour-coated candle • soft pencil • bradawl • brush

1 Lightly draw your design onto the surface of the candle. If you are not very confidant about your artistic skills and would prefer not to work freehand, you can transfer a design from a book, magazine or piece of fabric, using tracing or carbon paper.

2 With the bradawl, trace over the design, making the cutting line deep enough to reveal the natural wax beneath the coloured layer, and keeping the cutting depth uniform. Work your way over the entire design, brushing away unwanted wax shavings as you go to keep the design clean.

Appliquéd candles

plain candle • ready-made coloured wax sheet • hairdryer • greaseproof paper • pastry cutters • craft knife • wax glue • ovenproof bowl • saucepan • paint brush

1 Place a bowl in a pan of simmering water. Add a little wax glue to the bowl and allow it to melt.

2 Place a wax sheet on a piece of greaseproof paper and warm it with a hairdryer to soften it slightly. Using a sharp knife or pastry cutter, cut out your chosen motifs. Keep the shapes simple for the best effect.

3 While the wax motifs are still soft, brush the surface of the candle with molten wax glue.

4 Carefully pick up a motif on your knife and place in position on the candle. Press the motif firmly in place. Repeat the process with the remaining motifs.

Decoupage candles

plain candle • decorative items • wax glue • paint brush • paraffin wax • double burner • baking tray • greaseproof paper

1 Melt a little wax glue and, using a brush, paint it onto the surface of the candle. Working quickly, before the glue has time to set, press the decorative items firmly in place and leave the glue to dry.

2 To protect delicate items, melt a little paraffin wax in a double burner then pour it into a baking tray lined with greaseproof paper. When the wax has spread, roll the decorated candle in the wax and set it aside to dry.

Colour-coated candles

Although most candles are coloured as they are being made, by adding crushed, powdered dye to the molten wax, plain candles can also be colour-coated by dipping them in a thin layer of dyed molten wax. Candles can be overdipped completely, or a small section immersed to achieve a two-tone effect. For a quick and inexpensive alternative, try melting non-toxic wax crayons in an ovenproof dish (these can also be used to paint candles), but be warned: crayon wax may make the wick spit slightly when it is burnt.

plain candle • wax dye • paraffin wax • dipping can

1 Place the wax in the dipping can and heat it to 82°C (177°F). Add the crushed dye to the molten wax and stir thoroughly until the dye is thoroughly blended.

2 Dip the candle into the wax two or three times, leaving around 30 seconds between each dip to allow each coat to set. After the final coat, hang the candle to allow it to dry evenly.

Quick container candles

If time is against you, here is an idea for handmade candles that won't take all day.

inexpensive plain candles • ovenproof jug • scent (optional) • primed container wick • wicking needle • container of your choice

1 Place the candles in an ovenproof jug and melt them in a hot oven. Remove the old wicks from molten wax. The scent of your choice can be added at this stage if required – blend it thoroughly with the wax. Pour it carefully into your chosen container.

2 When the wax is nearly set but still soft enough to work, make a straight hole vertically through the centre of the candle using a wicking needle. Push the wick down into the wax.

3 As the candle cools, you might find that the wax level drops slightly, forming a dip in the surface. To correct this, simply top up the container with a little more molten wax and then leave it to set until it is completely hard.

GLOSSARY

CANDLES

From plain white utilitarian candles to the most colourful and intricate of moulded designs, there's a candle for every occasion.

Beeswax candles

Beeswax candles burn slowly and clearly, with a wonderful honey aroma. Having been removed from the hive and separated from the honey it contains, the wax can be melted down or cut into thin sheets and rolled around a wick. Pure molten beeswax can be difficult to mould, so traditional production methods involve dipping or rolling. Although more expensive than paraffin wax, beeswax does lengthen the burning time of a candle. For this reason it is often added to paraffin wax to improve the quality of the resulting moulded or dipped candle.

Church candles

Traditionally made from a high proportion of beeswax, church candles have survived unchanged for centuries. An integral part of religious ceremonies, these classic ivory pillars symbolize purity, life, the soul, faith and the love of God for man.

Dipped candles

This is the oldest form of candlemaking dating back to Roman times. The process involves repeatedly immersing a long wick into molten wax. The wax is left to dry after each dip so that the layers gradually build up to form the candle. Generally made in pairs so that the looped wick between the two acts as a handle for dipping, these candles have a tapered shape and an uneven base.

Floating candles

These short, broad-based, simply shaped candles use the water's reflective qualities to enhance the flickering light. The water remains clear as the candles burn, as its cool temperature prevents the hot molten wax from spreading. This is one of the safest ways to display candles.

Outdoor candles and flares

Garden candles usually take the form of container candles and have extra-thick wicks that are less likely to blow out. They can be made using ordinary paraffin wax or impregnated with citronella, a natural insect repellent. Brightly coloured flares, which burn for three hours or more depending on the wind, are also available. These are attached to sticks that can be pushed into the ground.

Scented candles

Candles that have scented oils added to them will fill a room with fragrance as they burn. Scented candles are normally moulded and, as perfume oils can make the wax more liquid, it is a good idea to stand them in a container large enough to hold the melted wax. A huge variety of scents are now available, from those that conjure up romance or relaxation to those that invigorate or refresh.

Straight-sided and moulded candles

The introduction of stearin in the early nineteenth century saw candlemaking change forever. A shrinking agent for wax, stearin enables candles to be moulded around a wick. This allowed candles to be produced in infinite varieties and shapes; it also resulted in candles of far higher quality, which burnt with a steady flame and were less prone to dripping.

Tallow candles

Made of wax extracted from beef or mutton fat, these candles, which are made using the dipping method, were the main source of artificial light for centuries. The tallow produces a foul smell when burnt and most of the light shed by the flame is obscured by smoke.

Tapers

These long, slender candles are essentially church candles that were held during religious processions.

Tealights

These small inexpensive candles are contained within a foil cup and have a surprisingly long burning time.

STORING CANDLES

• It is preferable to store candles in a horizontal position. Alternatively, place them upright in a candle box, but pack them together to avoid any bending should they become soft.
• Pairs of dipped candles can be stored decoratively, by simply hanging them over hooks.
• Always keep candles out of direct sunlight as they can melt and distort, while coloured candles may also fade.

CANDLE SNUFFERS

• When held over a lit candle, a snuffer starves the flame of oxygen and extinguishes it immediately.
• Snuffers reduce the smoky smells of extinguished candles.
• They also prevent molten wax from being blown onto surrounding surfaces.

HOLDERS

Aesthetic as well as practical, candle holders are as important a part of the display as the candle itself.

Candelabra

Usually made from metal, candelabras were originally made to hold ceremonial church candles. Designed for the table or floor-standing, they consist of arms or branches that hold two or more candles and provide a substantial source of light.

Ceramic candle holders

There are few surviving antique ceramics, but most potteries still produce a wide range, many of which are designed to match existing tableware designs. Traditionally, ceramic candlesticks took the form of classical pillars, as this shape was guaranteed to withstand the firing process. Since the eighteenth century more intricate designs have been made.

Chandeliers

The word chandelier comes from the French; it literally means candle holder, and refers to any holder with two or more candles (usually fashioned from wood, metal or glass). In the twelfth century, they consisted of huge iron or brass hoops hung in churches; the seventeenth century saw the manufacturer of S-shaped arms, usually arranged in groups of eight; while in the eighteenth century cut-glass chandeliers became popular. Many designs incorporate drip trays around each candle, but it is still advisable to use long-burning, non-drip candles.

Glass candle holders

Moulded glass saw a revival in the early nineteenth century, while the Victorians favoured cut and pressed glass, both clear and in delicate colours. Both used shape and pattern to catch and enhance light. Hand-blown glass can be shaped to any design and is characterized by its distinctive air bubbles. Coloured glassware is most effective when used to contain a candle, as the flame will glow through the glass bringing the colour to life.

Lanterns

Traditionally an iron frame with glass panels, lanterns are ideal for outdoor use as they protect the flame from draughts. Glass candle lamps, where the flame is protected by a globe or bowl of clear, etched or coloured glass, were used in the home, and these were the forerunner of the paraffin lamp.

Metal candle holders

The fact that metal is durable and fire resistant make it the ideal, and traditional, material for making candlesticks. It can be worked into any design, from delicate filigree to sturdy floor-standing pillars. Metals used include cast iron, pewter, silver, copper and brass, with each one bringing its own distinctive colour and qualities to a design. The popularity of metal candlesticks was at its height in the eighteenth century.

Nightlights

Used to hold tealights, these small containers are designed to protect the flame. They are traditionally round and made from glass or metal, such as brass or steel. Glass nightlights can be clear or coloured, while the metal variety often have patterned holes punched into the sides to allow the flame to shine out.

Sconces

First seen in the seventeenth century and designed to be fixed to a wall, sconces originally incorporated a highly polished metal backplate (later replaced with mirror glass) that helped to increase the amount of light shed by the single candle. In the eighteenth century the reflectors were removed and more candles added to increase light output. The backplate was replaced by ornate, picturesque detailing.

Wooden candle holders

Originating from the Medieval custom of supporting a candle with a spike pushed into the top of a block of wood or post, wooden candlesticks have a solid and enduring quality, and will sit comfortably in almost any setting. A highly versatile medium, wood can be turned, painted, carved or embellished.

DIRECTORY

UK

Aromatherapy Associates
Head office: 68 Maltings
Place, Bagleys Lane,
London SW6 2BY
Tel 020 7371 9878
*Makers of high-quality
aromatherapy products,
including candles and
essential oils.*

Aromatique
154 Brompton Road,
London SW3 1HX
Tel 020 7351 1950
*Founded in 1982 and sold
in over 40 countries, this top
American range includes
hand-poured candles.*

L'Artisan Parfumeur
17 Cale Street,
London SW3 3QR
Tel 020 7352 4196
*A wide range of candles
and essential oils designed
to create an atmosphere.*

Aveda Institute
28 Marylebone High
Street, London W1M 3PF
Tel 020 7224 3157
*The Aveda home range
includes candles and
diffuser oils in five natural
plant-based perfumes. The
hand-poured plant pure-
fume candles are available
in five natural aromas.*

Candle Makers Suppliers
28 Blythe Road,
London W14 0PP
Tel 020 7602 4031
*All the equipment and
materials necessary for
making candles. A mail
order service is available.*

Suzie Clayton
2 St Margarets Business
Centre, Moor Mead Road,
Twickenham TW1 1JS
Tel 020 8607 9704
*Established in 1990, Suzie
Clayton designs and makes
fine quality candle shades,
lamps and lampshades.*

Colony Gift Corporation Ltd
Lindal-in-Furness, Ulverston,
Cumbria LA12 0LD
Tel 01229 461100
*Established in 1979,
Colony is one of
the largest candle
manufacturers and
suppliers in Britain.
They produce a vast
range of candles,
accessories, oil burners
and scented products.
They produce the widest
range of scented candles
in the country.*

Crabtree & Evelyn
6 Kensington Church
Street, London W8 4EP
Tel 020 7937 9335
*For other shops and
stockists phone head
office on 020 7603 1611
A wide variety of aromatic
products for the home.
The scented candles are
of excellent quality.*

Czech & Speake
125 Fulham Road,
London SW3 6RT
Tel 020 7225 3667
*Initially founded in 1976
as a purveyor of bathroom
fittings and accessories,
Czech & Speake offers
a range of room sprays,
as well as fragrant
candles, vaporizing oils
and burning sticks.*

Floris
89 Jermyn Street,
London SW1Y 6JH
Tel 020 7930 2885
*'Floris At Home', a
coordinated range of
home fragrance products,
was launched in 1999 and
features top-quality candles
(containing 10 per cent
pure fragrance). There are
five scents to choose from
– Seasonal Spice, Jasmine
& Rose, Hyacinth & Bluebell,
Aromatic Lavender and
Oriental Bouquet.*

Homecrafts Direct
PO Box 38, Leicester LE1 9BU
Tel 0116 251 3139
*A mail-order service
supplying everything you
need to make candles,
including wax, beeswax
sheets, moulds, wicks,
stearin, dyes and perfume.*

Jurlique
Apotheke 2020,
296 Chiswick High Road,
London W4 1PA
Tel 020 8995 2293
*In addition to organic
essential oils from
Australia, Jurlique also
offers specially blended
mood-enhancing oils for
vaporizing. These include
Party Blend (geranium,
ylang ylang, orange
and rose), Romance
Blend (ylang ylang,
orange and patchouli)
and Clarity (lemon,
orange, bergamot,
pine and lavender).*

Kirker Greer & Co
Belvedere Road,
Burnham-on-Crouch,
Essex CM0 8AJ
Tel 01621 784647
*Kirker Greer started life
on the kitchen table of
a Georgian school house
in Essex. This family-run
business produces fine
beeswax candles and
scented candles from
their own hives.*

Jo Malone
150 Sloane Street,
London SW1X 9BX
Tel 020 7730 2100
*This fashionable perfumer
sells a range of luxuriously
scented candles, many of
which match her colognes.*

L'Occitane
67 King's Road,
London SW3 4NT
Tel 020 7823 4555
For mail order and other

stores and stockists,
call 020 7290 1421
*The scented candles are
stylishly packaged in tins.
There are many delicious
and unusual fragrances
to choose from, such as
Apricot and Grapefruit,
Tomato and Blackcurrant
and Orange Nutmeg,
all inspired by the fruits,
flowers, herbs and spices
of the markets of Provence.*

Penhaligon's
18 Beauchamp Place,
London SW3 1NQ
Tel 020 7584 4008
For shops and stockists,
call 0800 716 108
*Founded in 1870,
Penhaligon's specializes
in old-fashioned floral
fragrances, such as
Elizabethan Rose, Bluebell
and English Fern. The
candles are of unbeatable
quality and are packed
with enough scent to
perfume an entire room.*

Price's candles
110 York Road,
London SW11 3RU
Tel 020 7228 3345
*Established in 1830, Price's
Candles manufacture a
wide range of candles
and accessories, including
aromatherapy candles.*

Space NK
127–31 Westbourne
Grove, London W2 4UP
Tel 020 7727 8002
For shops and stockists,
call 020 7299 4999
*Stocks a great range of
home fragrance products
ranging from Diptyque
and other designer
candles to its own brand,
Space.NK.Home.*

St Eval Candle Company
Engollan, St Eval, Wadebridge,
Cornwall PL27 7UL
Tel 01841 540850

*Fine quality handmade
candles and church candles.*

Wax Lyrical
Head office:
4b Swallowfield Way,
Hayes, Middlesex UB3 1DQ
Tel 020 8561 0235
*A wide range of candles
and candle holders.*

FRANCE

L'Artisan Parfumeur
24 Boulevard Raspail,
75007 Paris
Tel (33) 1 42 22 23 32
See above.

Diptyque
34 boulevard Saint-
Germain, 75005 Paris
Tel (33) 1 43 26 45 27
*In 1961 English painter
Desmond Knox-Leet opened
a boutique in Paris offering
the first 'Made in England'
potpourris, pomanders and
perfumed candles. The
candles now come in over
30 different fragrances.*

Parfums Rigaud
Head office: 9 rue Saint-
Florentin, 75008 Paris
Tel (33) 1 42 60 11 14
*Rigaud candles date back
to 1950; they are entirely
handmade and regarded
as the best scented
candles in the world.*

USA

L'Artisan Parfumeur
870 Madison Avenue,
New York, NY 10021
Tel (1) 212 517 8665
See above.

Aveda Lifestyle Store
509 Madison Avenue,
New York, NY 10022
Tel (1) 212 832 2416
See above.

Banana Republic
552 Broadway, New York,
NY 10012
Tel (1) 212 925 0308

*The new home range
includes beautiful scented
candles – called Beach
House or Casablanca Lilies.*

Candles Plus
227 South 3rd Street,
Geneva, IL 60134
Tel (001) 630 262 2570
*A dazzling array of
candles and accessories.*

Candlestick
1817th Avenue, New York,
NY 10011
Tel (1) 212 924 5444
*A vast array of ready-
made candles, plus
everything you need to
make your own candles.*

Coty
Head office: 1325 6th
Avenue, New York,
NY 10019
Tel (1) 212 479 4300
*Scented candles containing
natural botanical extracts.*

Floris of London
703 Madison Avenue,
New York, NY 10021
Tel (1) 212 935 9100
See above.

Fresh
57 Spring Street,
New York, NY 10013
Tel (1) 212 925 0099
*Quirky home fragrance
products, including orange-
chocolate candles, as well
as more traditional products
such as Linden & Wisteria
and Sweet Pea candles.*

L'Occitane
For mail order and stockists,
call (1) 203 629 0885
See above.

Perfumes Isabell
Head office:30 West 26th
Street, New York, NY 10010
Tel (1) 212 647 7500
*The mood-enhancing
candles are favoured by
the rich and famous.*

INDEX

ACKNOWLEDGEMENTS

The author would like to Thank the following for their contributions to *Candles*: Lizzie Orme for her ever-beautiful photography and Lisa Brown for her stunning styling; Petra Boase for her innovative and stylish projects; project editor Zia Mattocks for all her hard work, and all those who took the time and trouble to provide information for this book, especially Amanda Cocks at Colony Candles.

Thanks also to my daughter, who, at the tender age of two, spent many evenings sitting patiently by a computer; and friends and fellow journalists Anna Lisa De'Ath and Jane Burdon for their help and support.

A special thank you to Helen Stone who first put me in touch with the talented Carlton team.

The publishers would like to thank the following people for allowing us to photograph in their beautiful homes: Abigail Ahern (pages 4–5, 7 top right and centre right, 24, 30, 31, 42–3, 44, 47, 48 bottom, 49, 55, 56 right, 95, 105, 132, 134, 137 and 139), architect Matthew Priestman, interior styling Abigail Ahern; and Laura Govett (pages 7 bottom right, 8–9, 14, 56 top left, 72 right, 74, 75, 82 and 101), architect Jonathan Clarc, interior design Laura Govett.

Additional photography by Polly Wreford, Graham Atkins-Hughes, Janine Hosegood, Tom Leighton, Mel Yates and Catherine Gratwicke.